# ECG IN EMERGENCY

## ECG READING MADE EASY

## DR CHARAN S YELANADU

Made with ♥ on the Notion Press Platform
www.notionpress.com

# Contents

# Foreword

In an emergency situation, the ability to quickly and accurately interpret an electrocardiogram (ECG) can mean the difference between life and death. The ECG is a powerful diagnostic tool, offering insights into the heart's electrical activity that can guide critical decisions. However, its complexity often poses a challenge, even for seasoned professionals. This book aims to demystify the ECG and help students understand ECG in simplified manner to have the knowledge and confidence they need to utilize this tool effectively.

When i was posted in Casualty posting during my internship, the ECG was an intimidating aspect of my practice. The myriad of waveforms, intervals, and segments seemed like an intricate puzzle that required deciphering under immense pressure. Over time, and with the guidance of experienced mentors, I began to appreciate the nuances of ECG interpretation. This book is a culmination of that journey, distilled into a practical guide that blends theory with real-world application.

My approach in this book is straightforward: we start with the basics and build up to more complex scenarios. Each chapter is designed to be both educational and accessible, whether you are a medical student just starting out or an experienced practitioner looking for a refresher. We cover a broad spectrum of topics, from the foundational principles of ECG interpretation to the recognition of life-threatening conditions such as myocardial infarction, arrhythmias, and electrolyte imbalances.

I have included numerous case studies and practical examples that reflect the high-stakes environment of emergency care. These scenarios are designed to simulate real-life situations, helping you to hone your skills and apply your knowledge effectively.

As you navigate through the chapters, you will find that the ECG is not just a diagnostic tool but a language—a language that speaks volumes about the heart's condition. By the end of this book, our goal is for you to be fluent in this language, able to interpret its signals with precision and confidence.

I would like to extend my gratitude to the many colleagues and mentors who have contributed to this work, and to the countless patients who have taught me invaluable lessons over the years.

*Dr. Charan S Yelanadu*
*30/07/2024*

# Preface

In an emergency care, every second counts. The ability to swiftly and accurately interpret an electrocardiogram (ECG) can be pivotal in diagnosing and managing life-threatening conditions. This book, "ECG in Emergency," is born out of a deep recognition of the crucial role that ECGs play in emergency medical settings and the need for a comprehensive, yet accessible, guide to mastering this essential skill.

My journey with the ECG began during my early years as a medical student. Like many, I was initially overwhelmed by the complex waveforms and the plethora of information an ECG could reveal. Over time, with guidance from mentors and countless hours of practice, I came to appreciate the ECG not just as a diagnostic tool, but as a vital language of the heart that, when understood, could save lives.

This book is the culmination of my experiences, insights, and the lessons learned throughout my career. It is designed to be a practical resource for medical students, residents, and seasoned practitioners alike. Whether you are encountering the ECG for the first time or seeking to deepen your existing knowledge, this book aims to provide a clear, systematic approach to ECG interpretation in the emergency setting.

We shall begin with the foundational principles of ECG interpretation, ensuring that you have a solid understanding of the basics. From there, we delve into more complex topics, including the recognition of various cardiac conditions such as myocardial infarction, arrhythmias, and electrolyte imbalances. Each chapter builds upon the last, with a focus on practical application and real-world scenarios.

Throughout the book, you will find numerous case studies and examples drawn from my own experiences and those of my colleagues. These cases are designed to help you to develop the skills and confidence needed to interpret ECGs accurately and efficiently under pressure.

One of the key themes of this book is the importance of context in ECG interpretation. In the emergency setting, an ECG cannot be viewed in isolation; it must be considered alongside the patient's clinical presentation and history. This holistic approach is emphasized throughout the chapters, reinforcing the critical thinking and decision-making skills that are essential for effective emergency care.

I owe a debt of gratitude to my mentors, colleagues, and students, whose questions, insights, and feedback have shaped the content of this book. I am also deeply grateful to the patients who have entrusted me with their care, providing invaluable lessons that have enriched my understanding of the ECG.

It is my sincere hope that "ECG in Emergency" will serve as a valuable resource, guiding you through the complexities of ECG interpretation and enhancing your ability to provide timely, effective care to your patients.

*Dr. Charan S Yelanadu*
*30/07/2024*

# Acknowledgements

The journey of writing "ECG in Emergency" has been a deeply rewarding experience, and it would not have been possible without the support and contributions of many individuals. I would like to take this opportunity to express my heartfelt gratitude to all those who have played a role in bringing this book to fruition.

First and foremost, I extend my deepest appreciation to my mentors, who have guided me throughout my career and instilled in me a passion for ECG interpretation. Their wisdom, encouragement, and unwavering support have been invaluable, and I am forever grateful for their mentorship.

I am also immensely thankful to my colleagues and peers in the field of General Medicine. Your collaboration, insights, and feedback have been instrumental in shaping the content of this book. The countless discussions, case reviews, and shared experiences have enriched my understanding and have significantly contributed to the depth and quality of this work.

To the medical students and residents I have had the privilege of teaching, thank you for your curiosity, enthusiasm, and dedication. Your questions and eagerness to learn have inspired me to continually refine my own knowledge and teaching methods. This book is, in many ways, a reflection of our shared learning journey.

I would like to acknowledge the contributions of the patients who have entrusted me with their care. Your courage and resilience have taught me invaluable lessons, and your experiences have provided the real-world context that is so crucial to the practice of General Medicine.

To my family and friends, thank you for your unwavering support, patience, and understanding throughout the writing process. Your encouragement and belief in me have been a source of strength and motivation, and I could not have completed this book without you.

Finally, I would like to express my gratitude to all the readers of this book. It is my hope that "ECG in Emergency" will serve as a valuable resource, enhancing your understanding and proficiency in ECG interpretation, and ultimately, improving patient care in emergency settings.

*Dr. Charan S Yelanadu*
*30/07/2024*

# Prologue

The emergency care is a place where time and precision converge, where every decision can have profound consequences. Among the many tools at the disposal of an emergency medical professional, the electrocardiogram (ECG) stands out as a critical instrument in the diagnostic arsenal. Its ability to provide real-time insights into the heart's electrical activity makes it indispensable in the fast-paced environment of emergency medicine.

The genesis of "ECG in Emergency" lies in my own experiences and challenges faced in the emergency department. Early in my career, I was often overwhelmed by the intricacies of ECG interpretation. The myriad waveforms and the urgent need to decipher them quickly under immense pressure were daunting. However, these challenges also fueled my determination to master the ECG and share that knowledge with others who find themselves in similar situations.

This book is not just a technical manual; it is a narrative of the heartbeat in emergency care. It is a story of learning and growth, of the crucial moments when understanding an ECG can alter the course of a patient's life. Each chapter is crafted to bring clarity to the complexities of ECG interpretation, blending theoretical knowledge with practical application.

As you turn the pages of this book, you will be guided through the fundamentals of ECG interpretation and progressively introduced to more complex scenarios. You will encounter a variety of case studies that mirror real-life situations in the emergency care, providing you with the opportunity to apply what you have learned in a realistic context. These cases are designed to enhance your critical thinking and decision-making skills, ensuring that you are prepared for the myriad challenges that you may face.

One of the central themes of this book is the integration of clinical context with ECG interpretation. In emergency situation, an ECG cannot be interpreted in isolation; it must be understood in conjunction with the patient's symptoms, history, and overall clinical picture. This holistic approach is emphasized throughout the book, reinforcing the importance of comprehensive patient assessment in making accurate diagnoses.

Writing "ECG in Emergency" has been a labor of love, driven by a passion for teaching and a commitment to improving patient care. It is my hope that this book will serve as a beacon for medical professionals at all stages of their careers, guiding them through the complexities of ECG interpretation and empowering them to make life-saving decisions with confidence.

As you embark on this journey, I invite you to immerse yourself in the world of ECGs, to embrace the challenges and triumphs that come with mastering this vital skill. May this book inspire you, educate you, and ultimately enhance your ability to provide exceptional care.

*Dr. Charan S Yelanadu*
*30/07/2024*

# CHAPTER ONE

# INTRODUCTION

Electrocardiograms are a cornerstone of cardiac diagnostics, providing invaluable insights into the heart's electrical activity. Despite their importance, ECGs are often seen as complex and challenging to interpret, especially under the pressure of an emergency situation. This book aims to demystify the ECG and provide a clear, systematic approach to its interpretation, tailored specifically for the emergency context.

In an emergency situation who really cares about physiology and mechanism of ECG. This book is a Handy pocket note book just to help you perform and interpret ECG in a correct manner only.

**Why This Book?**

"ECG in Emergency" is born out of a need for a practical, accessible resource that addresses the unique challenges faced by emergency medical practitioners. Unlike general ECG textbooks, this book focuses on the conditions and scenarios most commonly encountered in the emergency care. From acute myocardial infarctions to life-threatening arrhythmias, the content is designed to be directly applicable to the high-pressure decisions you face daily.

**What You Will Learn**

This book is structured to guide you through the essentials of ECG interpretation and progressively introduce more complex concepts. Here's a brief overview of what you can expect:

1. **Fundamentals of ECG Interpretation:** We start with the basics, ensuring a solid understanding of the standard 12-lead ECG, its components, and the normal values.

2. **Common ECG Patterns:** The book delves into the identification and interpretation of common ECG patterns, such as normal sinus rhythm, atrial fibrillation, and ventricular tachycardia, among others.

3. **Emergency-Specific Scenarios:** Special emphasis is placed on conditions frequently encountered in the emergency care, including myocardial infarction, electrolyte imbalances, and drug-induced changes.

4. **Case Studies:** Real-world case studies are interspersed throughout the chapters, providing practical examples and reinforcing the application of theoretical knowledge.

5. **Critical Decision-Making:** We discuss strategies for making rapid, informed decisions based on ECG findings, integrating clinical context to enhance diagnostic accuracy.

### How to Use This Book

"ECG in Emergency" is designed to be both a learning tool and a reference guide. Each chapter builds on the previous one, but they can also stand alone, allowing you to focus on specific topics as needed. Whether you are a novice looking to build a strong foundation or an experienced practitioner seeking a refresher, this book is structured to meet your needs.

### A Personal Journey

Writing this book has been a deeply personal journey. My early experiences in the emergency department were filled with the anxiety and urgency that many of you may feel. Through years of practice, study, and the invaluable mentorship of colleagues, I developed a deep understanding and appreciation of the ECG. It is my hope that this book will pass on that knowledge, making the process of learning ECG interpretation smoother and more intuitive for you.

### The Road Ahead

As you embark on this journey through "ECG in Emergency," I encourage you to approach each chapter with curiosity and diligence. Mastering the ECG is a challenging but immensely rewarding endeavor. With practice and perseverance, the skills you develop will enhance your ability to deliver high-quality emergency care, ultimately improving patient outcomes.

Thank you for choosing this book as your guide. Together, we will navigate the complexities of the ECG, equipping you with the confidence and expertise to excel in ECG interpretation.

# CHAPTER TWO

# ECG BASICS

Understanding the electrocardiogram (ECG) is fundamental for any healthcare provider working in emergency care. The ECG provides a graphic representation of the heart's electrical activity and offers crucial insights into cardiac function. This chapter will cover the essential concepts and components of the ECG, ensuring a strong foundation for more advanced topics.

## 1.1 The Electrical Conduction System of the Heart

The heart's electrical conduction system ensures the coordinated contraction of the heart muscles. The key components include:

- **Sinoatrial (SA) Node:** The natural pacemaker of the heart, located in the right atrium. It initiates the electrical impulse that causes the heart to beat.

- **Atrioventricular (AV) Node:** Located between the atria and ventricles, it delays the impulse to allow the atria to contract fully before the ventricles contract.

- **Bundle of His:** A pathway that transmits impulses from the AV node to the ventricles.

- **Purkinje Fibers:** Networks of fibers that distribute the electrical impulse throughout the ventricles, ensuring synchronized contraction.

## 1.2 The ECG Paper

The ECG is recorded on graph paper that moves at a standard speed of 25 mm/second. The paper is divided into small and large squares, each representing a specific time and voltage.

- **Small Square:** 1 mm x 1 mm, representing 0.04 seconds (40 milliseconds) on the horizontal axis and 0.1 millivolts (mV) on the vertical axis.

- **Large Square:** 5 mm x 5 mm, representing 0.20 seconds (200 milliseconds) on the horizontal axis and 0.5 mV on the vertical axis.

### 1.3 ECG Leads

The standard 12-lead ECG consists of:

- **Limb Leads:** I, II, III, aVR, aVL, aVF

- **Precordial Leads:** V1, V2, V3, V4, V5, V6

Each lead views the heart from a different angle, providing a comprehensive view of the heart's electrical activity.

### 1.4 The ECG Waveforms

The ECG waveform consists of several key components:

- **P Wave:** Represents atrial depolarization. It is usually upright in most leads and lasts about 0.08 to 0.10 seconds.

- **PR Interval:** The time from the onset of the P wave to the start of the QRS complex, representing the time taken for the impulse to travel from the SA node to the ventricles. Normal duration is 0.12 to 0.20 seconds.

- **QRS Complex:** Represents ventricular depolarization. It normally lasts between 0.06 to 0.10 seconds. The QRS complex can vary in appearance but typically consists of a Q wave (initial downward deflection), R wave (upward deflection), and S wave (downward deflection following the R wave).

- **ST Segment:** The flat, isoelectric section of the ECG between the end of the S wave and the start of the T wave. It represents the period when the ventricles are depolarized.

- **T Wave:** Represents ventricular repolarization. It is typically upright in most leads.

- **QT Interval:** The time from the start of the QRS complex to the end of the T wave, representing the total time for ventricular depolarization and repolarization. The normal QT interval varies with heart rate but is generally less than 0.44 seconds.

- **U Wave:** A small wave that may follow the T wave, often seen in hypokalemia but not always present.

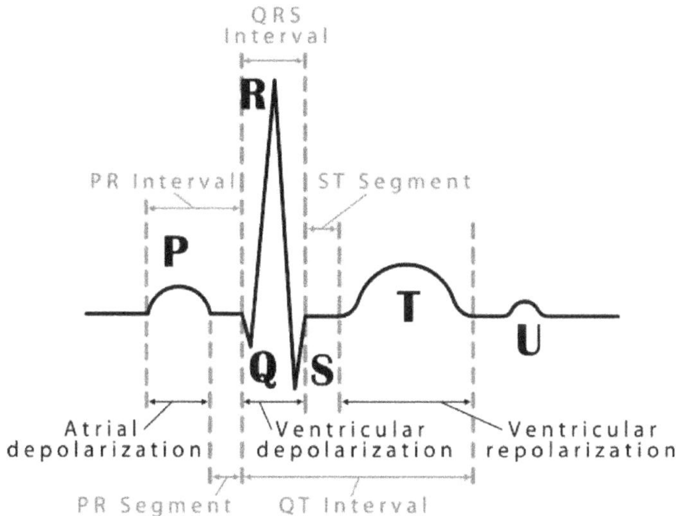


## 1.5 Systematic Approach to ECG Interpretation

A systematic approach ensures that no aspect of the ECG is overlooked. Follow these steps:

1. **Check the Patient's Details:** Verify the patient's name, age, and clinical context.

2. **Assess the Quality of the ECG:** Ensure the tracing is free from artifacts and properly calibrated.

3. **Determine the Heart Rate:** Count the number of R waves in a 6-second strip and multiply by 10, or use the large squares method (300/number of large squares between R waves).

4. **Analyze the Rhythm:** Determine if the rhythm is regular or irregular. Identify the presence of P waves, their relationship with the QRS complexes, and consistency.

5. **Examine the P Wave:** Assess the morphology, amplitude, and duration of the P wave in different leads.

6. **Measure the PR Interval:** Ensure it is within the normal range (0.12-0.20 seconds).

7. **Evaluate the QRS Complex:** Check the width and morphology of the QRS

complex. A normal QRS duration is 0.06-0.10 seconds.

8. **Inspect the ST Segment:** Look for any deviations from the isoelectric line, indicating ischemia or infarction.

9. **Assess the T Wave:** Evaluate the size, shape, and direction of the T wave.

10. **Measure the QT Interval:** Ensure it is appropriate for the heart rate (corrected QT interval, QTc, should be less than 0.44 seconds).

11. **Look for U Waves:** Note their presence and significance.

### 1.6 Common ECG Abnormalities

Understanding common ECG abnormalities is crucial for emergency medical practice:

- **Sinus Bradycardia:** Heart rate less than 60 bpm.
- **Sinus Tachycardia:** Heart rate more than 100 bpm.
- **Atrial Fibrillation:** Irregularly irregular rhythm with no distinct P waves.
- **Atrial Flutter:** Sawtooth pattern of atrial activity.
- **Ventricular Tachycardia:** Wide QRS complexes, rate typically between 150-250 bpm.
- **Ventricular Fibrillation:** Chaotic, irregular waveforms with no discernible QRS complexes.
- **Myocardial Infarction:** ST-segment elevation or depression, pathologic Q waves.
- **Bundle Branch Blocks:** Widened QRS complex with specific patterns in different leads.
- **Electrolyte Imbalances:** Peaked T waves in hyperkalemia, flattened T waves in hypokalemia, prolonged QT interval in hypocalcemia.

we shall discuss about the same in detail in coming chapters.

### 1.7 Conclusion

Mastering the basics of ECG interpretation is essential for any emergency medical practitioner. A systematic approach and a solid understanding of the heart's electrical activity and the components of the ECG waveform will enable you to make accurate and timely diagnoses, ultimately improving patient outcomes. As you progress through this book, you will build on this foundation, gaining the skills and confidence needed to excel in an emergency situation.

# CHAPTER THREE

# ECG LEADS AND PLACEMENT

The accurate placement of ECG leads is critical for obtaining a reliable and interpretable electrocardiogram. Each lead provides a unique view of the heart's electrical activity, and improper placement can lead to misinterpretation and potential diagnostic errors. This chapter will cover the different types of ECG leads, their specific placements, and the rationale behind their configurations.

### 2.1 Types of ECG Leads

The standard 12-lead ECG consists of three main types of leads:

1. Limb Leads
2. Augmented Limb Leads
3. Precordial (Chest) Leads

Each type of lead offers a different perspective on the heart's electrical activity, providing a comprehensive view when combined.

### 2.2 Limb Leads

There are three standard limb leads:

- **Lead I:** Records the electrical potential between the right arm (negative electrode) and the left arm (positive electrode).
- **Lead II:** Records the electrical potential between the right arm (negative electrode) and the left leg (positive electrode).
- **Lead III:** Records the electrical potential between the left arm (negative electrode) and the left leg (positive electrode).

**Placement:**

- Right Arm (RA): Electrode placed on the right wrist or right upper arm.
- Left Arm (LA): Electrode placed on the left wrist or left upper arm.
- Left Leg (LL): Electrode placed on the left ankle or left lower leg.

- Right Leg (RL): Electrode placed on the right ankle or right lower leg (used as a ground/reference electrode).

**Triangle Formation:**

These leads form Einthoven's Triangle, an imaginary equilateral triangle centered around the heart, with each side representing one of the bipolar limb leads.

### 2.3 Augmented Limb Leads

The augmented limb leads are unipolar and provide additional perspectives by using a single positive electrode and a combination of the other electrodes as a composite negative electrode.

- **aVR:** Right arm electrode is positive, and the combination of left arm and left leg electrodes form the negative.
- **aVL:** Left arm electrode is positive, and the combination of right arm and left leg electrodes form the negative.
- **aVF:** Left leg electrode is positive, and the combination of right arm and left arm electrodes form the negative.

**Placement:**

The electrode placement is the same as for the limb leads. The augmentation comes from the way the signals are processed, enhancing the view from the limb leads.

### 2.4 Precordial (Chest) Leads

The precordial leads provide a horizontal plane view of the heart and are crucial for localizing abnormalities within specific areas of the heart.

- **V1:** Fourth intercostal space to the right of the sternum.
- **V2:** Fourth intercostal space to the left of the sternum.
- **V3:** Midway between V2 and V4.
- **V4:** Fifth intercostal space at the midclavicular line.
- **V5:** Same level as V4, at the anterior axillary line.
- **V6:** Same level as V4, at the midaxillary line.

**Placement Tips:**

- Ensure precise placement by palpating the rib spaces and following anatomical landmarks.
- Proper lead placement is crucial for accurate diagnosis, especially in detecting conditions such as myocardial infarction.

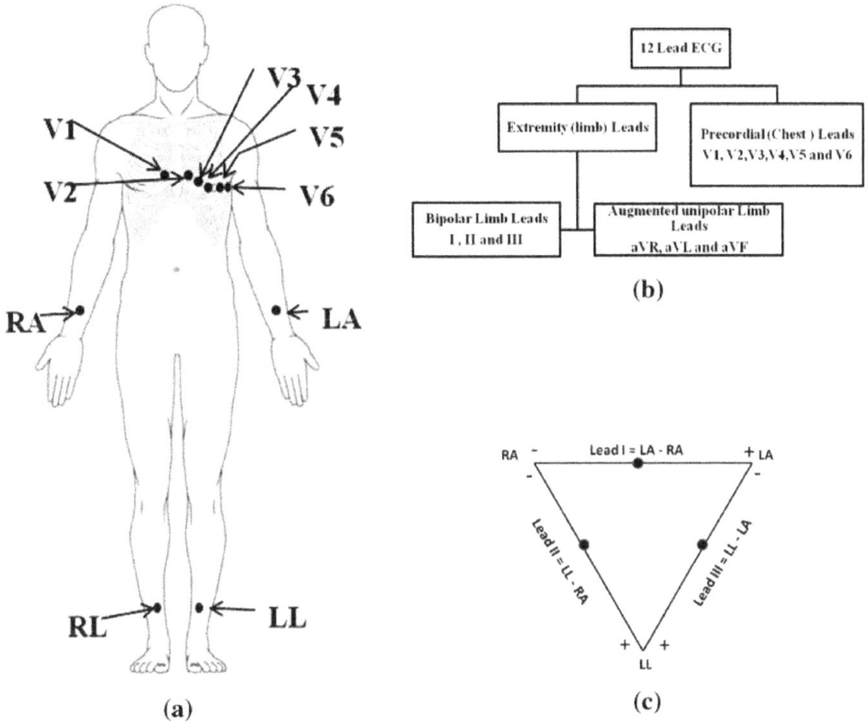



(a) Lead placements * (b) Leads* (c) Einthoven's Triangle*

## 2.5 Additional Leads

In certain clinical situations, additional leads may be used to provide more detailed information:

- **Right-sided Leads (V1R to V6R):** Similar to the standard precordial leads but placed on the right side of the chest. These are particularly useful for detecting right ventricular involvement in myocardial infarction.
- **Posterior Leads (V7 to V9):** Placed on the back (scapular and paraspinal areas) to assess posterior myocardial infarction.

## 2.6 Steps for Proper Lead Placement

1. Patient Preparation:
- Ensure the patient is relaxed and in a supine position.
- Clean the skin to remove oils and debris, which can affect electrode adhesion and signal quality.
- Shave any excessive chest hair if necessary.

2. Electrode Placement:

- Place the limb electrodes first to establish a baseline.

- Position the precordial leads accurately using anatomical landmarks.

- Double-check the placements to ensure they match the standardized positions.

3. Lead Connection:

- Connect the lead wires to the corresponding electrodes, ensuring no tension or pull on the wires that could displace the electrodes.

4. Verification:

- Verify the quality of the ECG tracing by checking for baseline wander, noise, or artifact.

- Reposition any electrodes if the signal is not clear.

## 2.7 Clinical Significance of Lead Views

Each lead provides a different perspective of the heart's electrical activity, aiding in the localization and diagnosis of various cardiac conditions:

- **Inferior Leads (II, III, aVF):** View the inferior wall of the left ventricle.

- **Lateral Leads (I, aVL, V5, V6):** View the lateral wall of the left ventricle.

- **Septal Leads (V1, V2):** View the interventricular septum.

- **Anterior Leads (V3, V4):** View the anterior wall of the left ventricle.

- **Right Ventricular Leads (Right-sided precordial leads):** View the right ventricle.

- **Posterior Leads (V7 to V9):** View the posterior wall of the left ventricle.

Understanding these views helps in diagnosing specific conditions such as myocardial infarctions, ischemia, and hypertrophy, allowing for more targeted and effective treatment.

## 2.8 Conclusion

Correct lead placement is foundational for obtaining accurate ECG readings. By adhering to standardized positions and understanding the perspectives each lead provides, healthcare professionals can effectively utilize the ECG to diagnose and manage a wide range of cardiac conditions. Mastery of lead placement and interpretation is essential for delivering high-quality emergency care and improving patient outcomes.

As you continue through this book, you will build upon these basics, learning to recognize and interpret the myriad of patterns and abnormalities that the ECG can reveal.

# CHAPTER FOUR

# NORMAL ECG PATTERNS

Understanding normal ECG patterns is crucial for identifying abnormalities and making accurate diagnoses. This chapter will provide a detailed overview of the characteristics of a normal ECG, including the P wave, PR interval, QRS complex, ST segment, T wave, QT interval, and U wave.

Electro-Cardio-Gram

**Normal 12-Lead ECG**

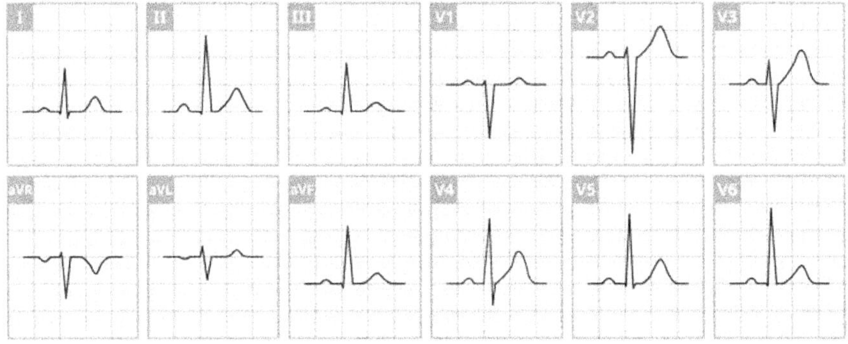

### 3.1 P Wave

The P wave represents atrial depolarization, which is the electrical activity that initiates atrial contraction.

**Characteristics:**

- Duration: 0.08 to 0.10 seconds (2-2.5 small squares on the ECG paper).
- Amplitude: Less than 0.25 mV (2.5 small squares).

- Morphology: Generally smooth and rounded.
- Direction: Typically upright in leads I, II, aVL, and V4-V6; inverted in lead aVR; variable in other leads.

**Significance:**

- The P wave should be consistent in shape and size throughout the ECG.
- Abnormal P waves can indicate atrial enlargement or other atrial abnormalities.

### 3.2 PR Interval

The PR interval represents the time taken for the electrical impulse to travel from the atria to the ventricles, encompassing atrial depolarization and the delay at the AV node.

**Characteristics:**

- Duration: 0.12 to 0.20 seconds (3-5 small squares).

**Significance:**

- A prolonged PR interval (>0.20 seconds) can indicate first-degree heart block.
- A shortened PR interval (<0.12 seconds) can be seen in pre-excitation syndromes such as Wolff-Parkinson-White (WPW) syndrome.

### 3.3 QRS Complex

The QRS complex represents ventricular depolarization, which triggers ventricular contraction.

**Characteristics:**

- Duration: 0.06 to 0.10 seconds (1.5-2.5 small squares).
- Amplitude: Varies depending on the lead; usually larger in chest leads due to their proximity to the heart.
- Morphology: Consists of three deflections:
- **Q wave:** The initial negative deflection.
- **R wave:** The first positive deflection.
- **S wave:** The negative deflection following the R wave.

**Significance:**

- A widened QRS complex (>0.12 seconds) suggests a conduction delay such as bundle branch block or ventricular rhythm.
- The presence of pathological Q waves (deeper and wider than normal) can indicate myocardial infarction.

### 3.4 ST Segment

The ST segment represents the period between the end of ventricular depolarization and the beginning of ventricular repolarization.

### Characteristics:
- Duration: Typically isoelectric (flat) and lasts around 0.08 to 0.12 seconds.
- Morphology: Should be level with the baseline of the PR segment.

### Significance:
- ST segment elevation or depression can indicate myocardial ischemia or infarction, pericarditis, or other cardiac conditions.

### 3.5 T Wave
The T wave represents ventricular repolarization.

### Characteristics:
- Duration: Varies, but the T wave is usually less than 0.20 seconds.
- Amplitude: Should be less than 5 mm in limb leads and less than 10 mm in precordial leads.
- Morphology: Generally upright and smooth in most leads; inverted in aVR.

### Significance:
- Abnormal T wave morphology (e.g., peaked, flattened, or inverted T waves) can indicate electrolyte imbalances, ischemia, or other cardiac conditions.

### 3.6 QT Interval
The QT interval represents the total time for ventricular depolarization and repolarization.

### Characteristics:
- Duration: Varies with heart rate, but generally less than 0.44 seconds. It is often corrected for heart rate (QTc) using formulas like Bazett's formula:

$$QTc = \frac{QT \text{ interval in seconds}}{\sqrt{\text{cardiac cycle in seconds}}} = \frac{QT}{\sqrt{RR}}$$

### Significance:
- A prolonged QT interval can increase the risk of ventricular arrhythmias and is seen in conditions such as Long QT Syndrome.
- A shortened QT interval can be associated with hypercalcemia and certain genetic conditions.

### 3.7 U Wave
The U wave is a small wave that follows the T wave and is thought to represent the repolarization of the Purkinje fibers.

**Characteristics:**

- Amplitude: Usually less than 1 mm.

- Morphology: Generally follows the direction of the T wave.

**Significance:**

- Prominent U waves can be seen in hypokalemia, bradycardia, and certain medications.

- Inverted U waves may indicate ischemia or left ventricular hypertrophy.

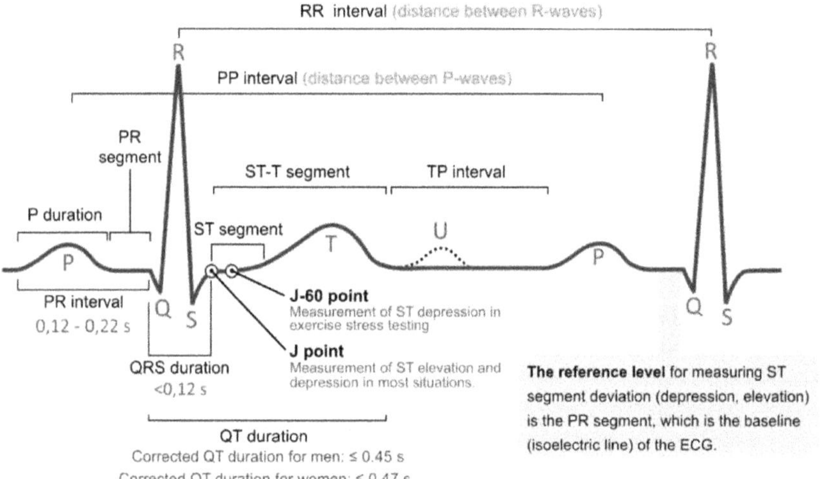


### 3.8 Analyzing a Normal ECG

A systematic approach to analyzing a normal ECG ensures that no aspect is overlooked:

1. **Check the Patient's Details:** Verify the patient's information and clinical context.

2. **Assess the Quality of the ECG:** Ensure there are no artifacts, and the paper speed is standard (25 mm/sec).

3. **Determine the Heart Rate:** Calculate using the R-R interval (300 divided by the number of large squares between R waves).

4. **Analyze the Rhythm:** Confirm it is regular and that each P wave is followed by a QRS complex.

5. **Examine the P Wave:** Check its shape, size, and consistency.

6. **Measure the PR Interval:** Ensure it is within the normal range.

7. **Evaluate the QRS Complex:** Confirm its duration and morphology.

8. **Inspect the ST Segment:** Look for any deviations from the baseline.

9. **Assess the T Wave:** Evaluate its size, shape, and direction.

10. **Measure the QT Interval:** Ensure it is appropriate for the heart rate.

11. **Look for U Waves:** Note their presence and significance.

### 3.9 Normal ECG Variants

Normal ECG patterns can vary based on several factors, including age, sex, and physical conditioning:

- **Pediatric ECGs:** Typically show faster heart rates and can have right ventricular dominance.

- **Athlete's Heart:** May show sinus bradycardia, a slightly prolonged PR interval, and early repolarization patterns.

- **Gender Differences:** Women may have shorter QT intervals than men.

### 3.10 Conclusion

Recognizing normal ECG patterns is the foundation for identifying and interpreting abnormalities. A thorough understanding of the normal characteristics of each ECG component will enable you to detect deviations and make informed clinical decisions. As you continue through this book, you will learn to identify and interpret a wide range of ECG abnormalities, enhancing your diagnostic skills and improving patient care in emergency settings.

# CHAPTER FIVE

# ABNORMAL ECG PATTERNS

Abnormal ECG patterns can indicate a variety of cardiac and systemic conditions. This chapter will cover a range of abnormal ECG patterns, including arrhythmias, conduction abnormalities, myocardial infarction, electrolyte imbalances, and drug effects. Understanding these patterns is crucial for making accurate diagnoses and providing timely treatment in emergency situations.

### 4.1 Arrhythmias

#### 4.1.1 Sinus Arrhythmia

**Characteristics:**

- Irregular R-R intervals.
- P waves are present before each QRS complex.

**Significance:**

- Often a normal finding, especially in young, healthy individuals.
- Can be exaggerated by changes in intrathoracic pressure during respiration.

## Sinus arrhythmia

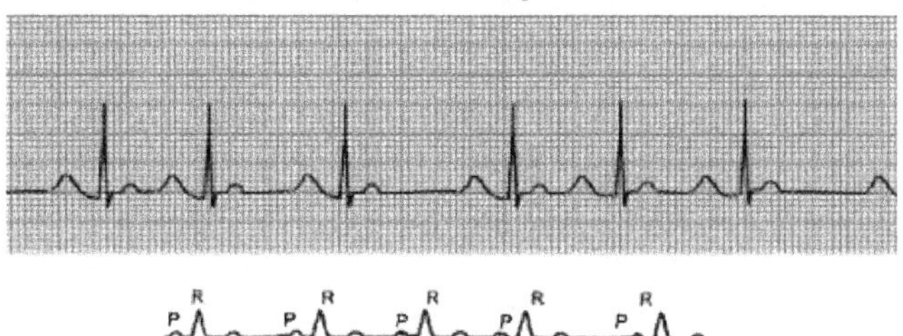



### 4.1.2 Sinus Bradycardia

**Characteristics:**

- Heart rate less than 60 beats per minute.
- Normal P waves, PR interval, and QRS complex.

**Significance:**

- Common in well-conditioned athletes.
- Can be due to increased vagal tone, hypothyroidism, hypothermia, or medications (e.g., beta-blockers).

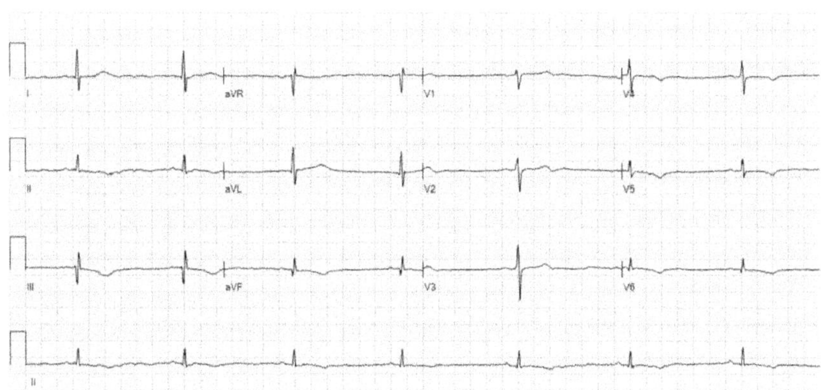

### 4.1.3 Sinus Tachycardia

**Characteristics:**

- Heart rate greater than 100 beats per minute.

- Normal P waves, PR interval, and QRS complex.

**Significance:**

- Normal physiological response to exercise, stress, or fever.

- Pathological causes include anemia, hyperthyroidism, hypovolemia, and heart failure.

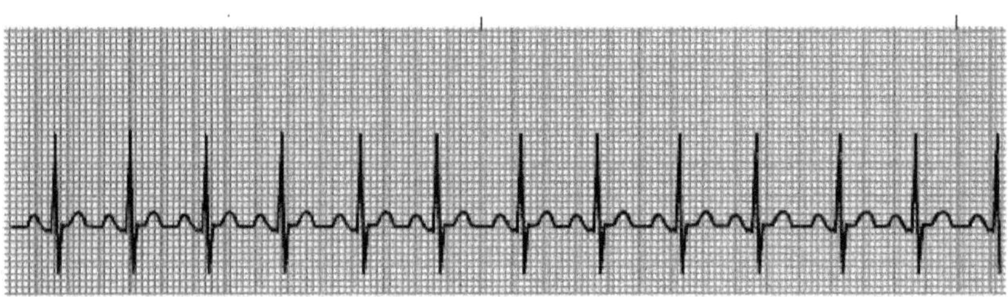

### *4.1.4 Atrial Fibrillation*

**Characteristics:**

- Irregularly irregular rhythm.

- No distinct P waves; presence of fibrillatory waves.

- Variable ventricular response.

**Significance:**

- Increased risk of thromboembolism and stroke.

- Associated with conditions like hypertension, valvular heart disease, and hyperthyroidism.

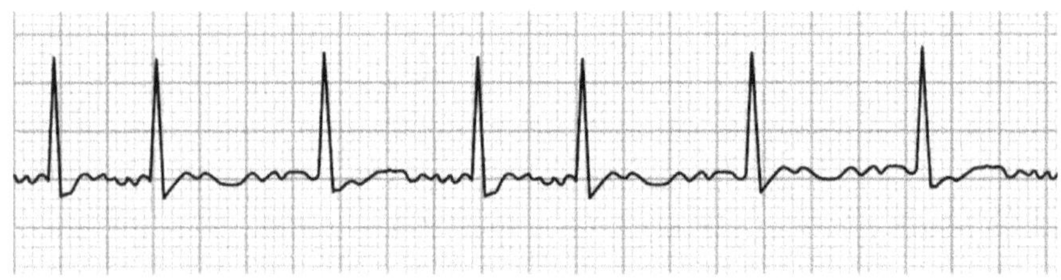

## Atrial Fibrillation Heart Rhythm

### 4.1.5 Atrial Flutter
**Characteristics:**
- Regular atrial activity with a sawtooth pattern, typically at a rate of 250-350 beats per minute.
- Ventricular response may be regular or irregular.
  **Significance:**
- Similar risk factors and complications as atrial fibrillation.
- Often requires rate control and anticoagulation therapy.

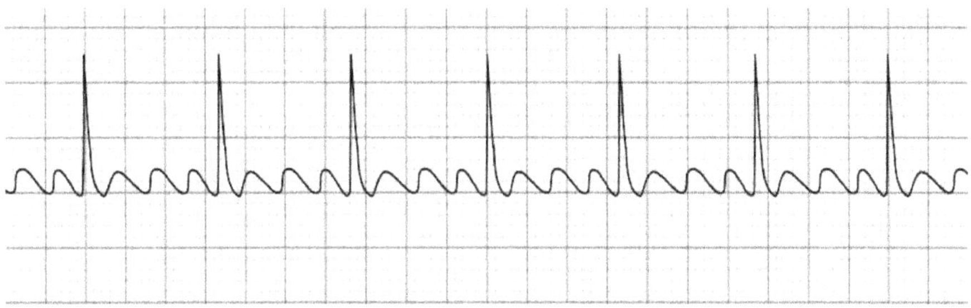

### 4.1.6 Supraventricular Tachycardia (SVT)
**Characteristics:**
- Regular, rapid heart rate typically between 150-250 beats per minute.
- P waves may be hidden in preceding T waves.
  **Significance:**
- Can cause palpitations, dizziness, and syncope.
- Often managed with vagal maneuvers, adenosine, or electrical cardioversion.

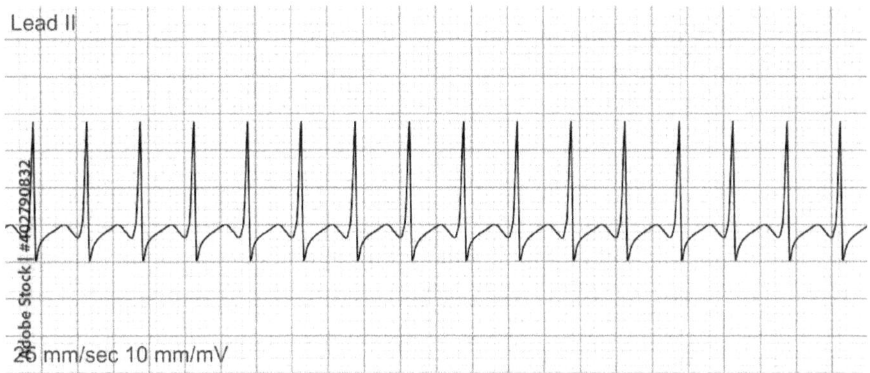

### *4.1.7 Ventricular Tachycardia (VT)*
**Characteristics:**

- Regular, wide QRS complexes (>0.12 seconds) with a rate of 100-250 beats per minute.
- P waves, if present, are dissociated from QRS complexes.

**Significance:**

- Life-threatening arrhythmia requiring immediate intervention.
- Commonly associated with ischemic heart disease, cardiomyopathy, and electrolyte disturbances.

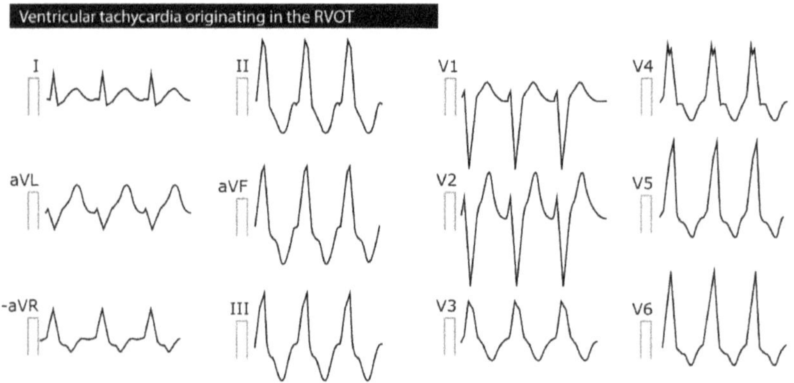


### *4.1.8 Ventricular Fibrillation (VF)*
**Characteristics:**

- Chaotic, irregular electrical activity with no discernible QRS complexes.
- No effective cardiac output.

**Significance:**

- Medical emergency requiring immediate defibrillation.
- Common cause of sudden cardiac death.

# Ventricular Fibrillation

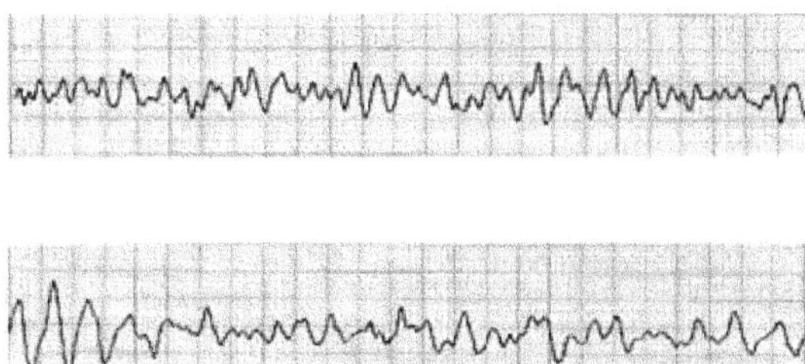

## 4.2 Conduction Abnormalities

### 4.2.1 First-Degree AV Block

**Characteristics:**

- Prolonged PR interval (>0.20 seconds).
- P waves precede each QRS complex.

**Significance:**

- Often benign but can indicate underlying heart disease.
- Can be caused by medications (e.g., beta-blockers, calcium channel blockers).

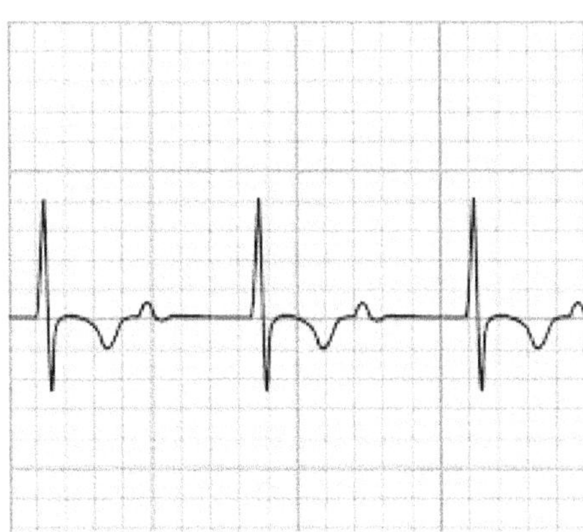

### 4.2.2 Second-Degree AV Block

**Mobitz Type I (Wenckebach):**
**Characteristics:**
- Progressive prolongation of the PR interval until a beat is dropped.
- Grouped beating.
   **Significance:**
- Usually benign and transient.
- May be associated with increased vagal tone or myocardial infarction.
   **Mobitz Type II:**
**Characteristics:**
- Sudden, non-conducted P waves without progressive PR prolongation.
- Constant PR intervals in conducted beats.
   **Significance:**
- More serious; can progress to third-degree AV block.
- Often requires pacemaker implantation.

**Mobitz I or Wenckebach**

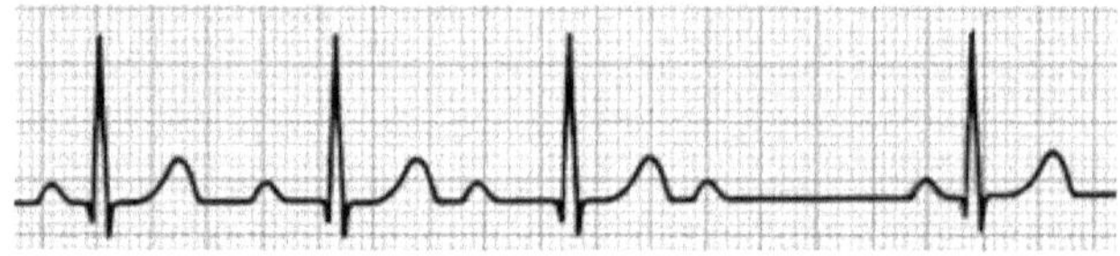

**Mobitz II**

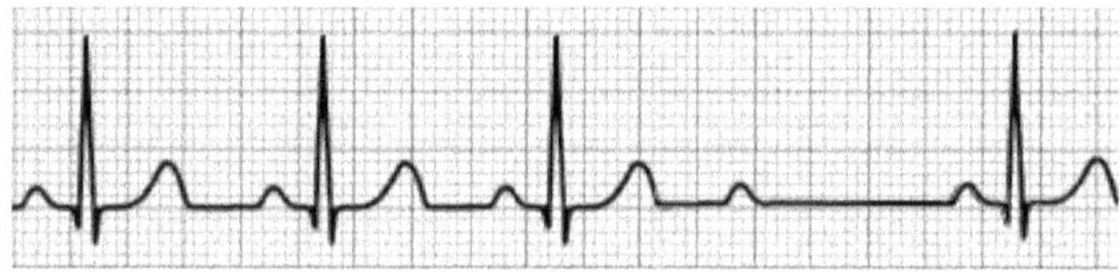

**2:1 block**

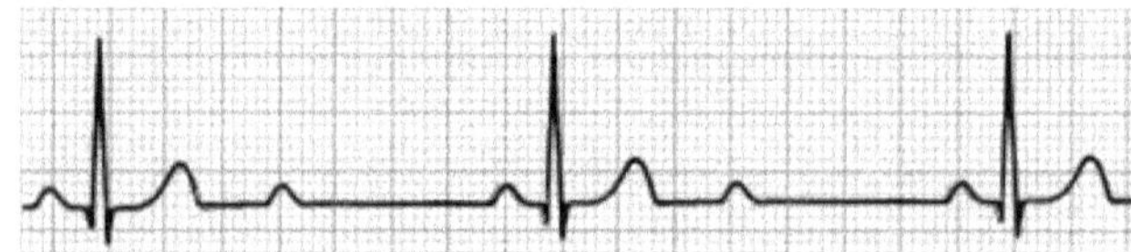

*4.2.3 Third-Degree (Complete) AV Block*
   **Characteristics:**
- No relationship between P waves and QRS complexes (AV dissociation).
- Atrial rate faster than ventricular rate.

**Significance:**

- Medical emergency often requiring pacemaker placement.
- Can result from ischemic heart disease, myocarditis, or drug toxicity.

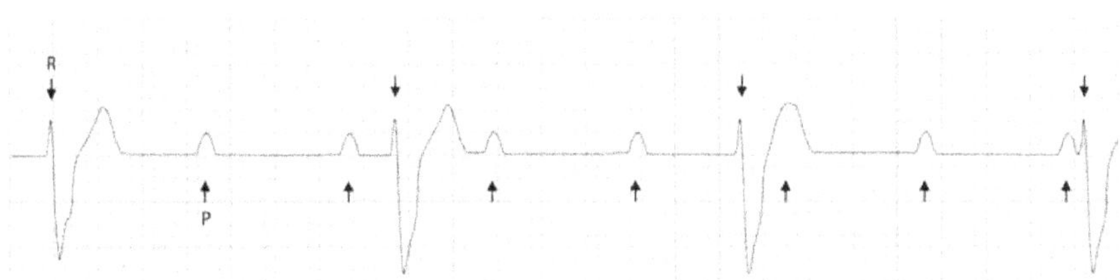

### 4.2.4 Bundle Branch Blocks

**Right Bundle Branch Block (RBBB):**

Characteristics:

- Wide QRS complex (>0.12 seconds).
- rsR' pattern in lead V1 (rabbit ears).
- Wide S wave in leads I and V6.

**Significance:**

- Can be benign or indicative of underlying heart disease.

**Left Bundle Branch Block (LBBB):**

Characteristics:

- Wide QRS complex (>0.12 seconds).
- Broad, notched R wave in leads I, aVL, V5, and V6.
- Deep S wave in leads V1 and V2.

**Significance:**

- Often associated with underlying cardiac pathology.
- Can obscure the diagnosis of myocardial infarction on ECG.

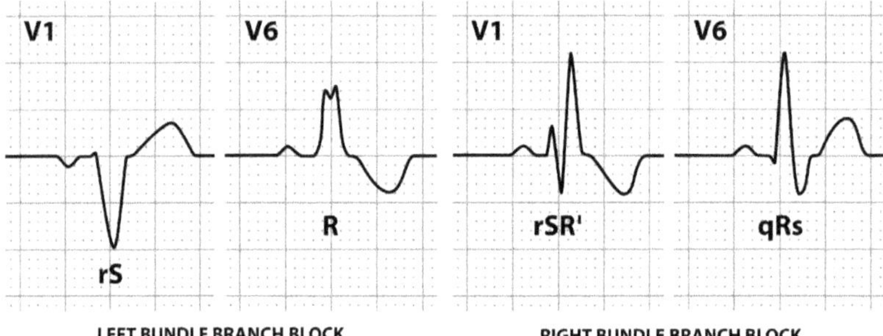



### 4.3 Myocardial Infarction

#### 4.3.1 ST-Segment Elevation Myocardial Infarction (STEMI)

**Characteristics:**

- ST-segment elevation in two or more contiguous leads.
- Reciprocal ST-segment depression in opposite leads.
- Pathological Q waves may develop over time.

**Significance:**

- Indicates acute myocardial infarction requiring urgent reperfusion therapy (e.g., PCI, thrombolysis).

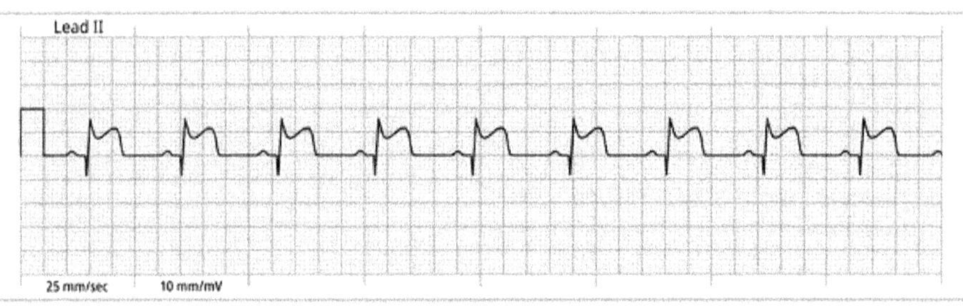



#### 4.3.2 Non-ST-Segment Elevation Myocardial Infarction (NSTEMI)

**Characteristics:**

- ST-segment depression or T-wave inversion in multiple leads.
- No ST-segment elevation.

**Significance:**

- Indicates myocardial ischemia without full-thickness infarction.
- Requires prompt medical management and risk stratification.

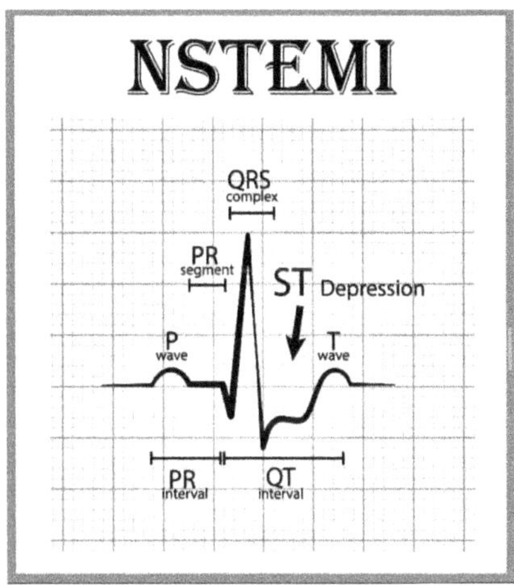


### 4.3.3 Q Waves

**Characteristics:**

- Pathological Q waves: >0.04 seconds wide and >2 mm deep or >25% of the subsequent R wave in height.

**Significance:**

- Indicate previous myocardial infarction.
- Presence of Q waves in specific leads can localize the infarction.

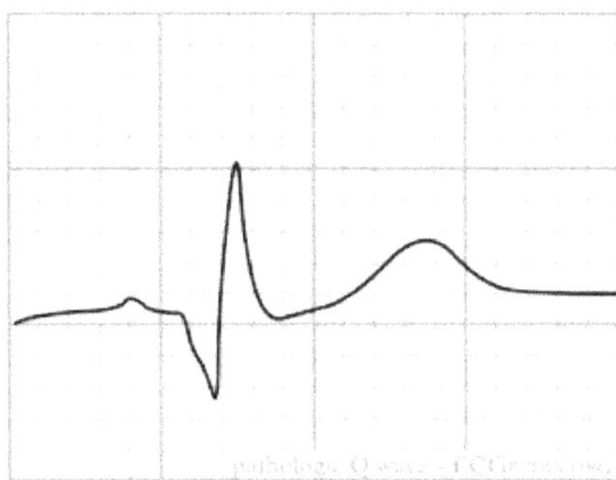

## 4.4 Electrolyte Imbalances

### 4.4.1 Hyperkalemia
**Characteristics:**
- Peaked T waves.
- Flattened P waves.
- Widened QRS complex.
- Sine wave pattern in severe cases.

**Significance:**
- Can lead to ventricular fibrillation and cardiac arrest.
- Requires urgent treatment with calcium, insulin, and glucose.

### 4.4.2 Hypokalemia
**Characteristics:**
- Flattened or inverted T waves.
- Prominent U waves.
- ST-segment depression.

**Significance:**
- Can cause arrhythmias such as torsades de pointes.
- Requires potassium replacement.

### 4.4.3 Hypercalcemia
**Characteristics:**
- Shortened QT interval.
- Osborn (J) waves in severe cases.

**Significance:**
- Associated with conditions such as hyperparathyroidism and malignancy.

### 4.4.4 Hypocalcemia
**Characteristics:**
- Prolonged QT interval.

**Significance:**
- Can lead to life-threatening arrhythmias.
- Requires calcium replacement.

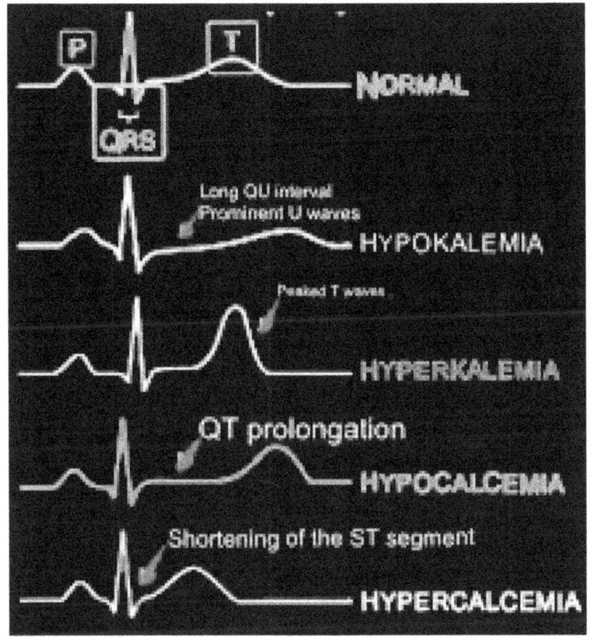


## 4.5 Drug Effects

### 4.5.1 Digoxin

**Characteristics:**

- Downsloping ST-segment depression (digoxin effect).
- Flattened or inverted T waves.
- Shortened QT interval.

**Significance:**

- Indicates therapeutic or toxic levels of digoxin.
- Toxicity can cause arrhythmias such as atrial tachycardia with block.

# Digoxin Effect

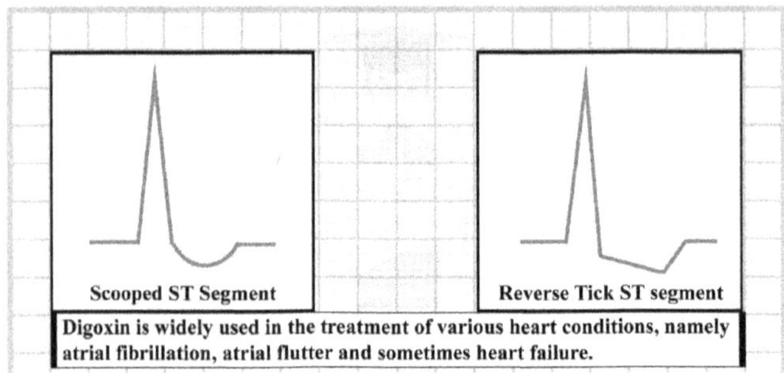



Digoxin is widely used in the treatment of various heart conditions, namely atrial fibrillation, atrial flutter and sometimes heart failure.

### 4.5.2 Antiarrhythmic Drugs

**Class IA (e.g., Quinidine):**

**Characteristics:**

- Prolonged QT interval.
- Wide QRS complex.

**Significance:**

- Risk of torsades de pointes.

**Class III (e.g., Amiodarone):**

**Characteristics:**

- Prolonged QT interval.

**Significance:**

- Risk of torsades de pointes.

### 4.5.3 Beta-Blockers and Calcium Channel Blockers

**Characteristics:**

- Sinus bradycardia.
- First-degree AV block.

**Significance:**

- Monitor for signs of overdose and hypotension.

**ANTIARRHYTHMIC DRUG ACTIONS**

| Vaughn-Williams Class | DRUG | ECG Changes | CHANNELS | | | RECEPTORS | | | | Clinical Effects | | | |
|---|---|---|---|---|---|---|---|---|---|---|---|---|---|
| | | | Ca$^{++}$ | Na$^+$ | K$^+$ | α | β | ACh | Ado | Pro-Arrhy | Extra Cardiac | LV FX | Heart Rate |
| I A | Quinidine | A | | (M) | (M) | (L) | | (M) | | (H) | (M) | | |
| | Procainamide | | | (M) | (M) | | | | | (M) | (H) | | |
| | Disopyramide (Norpace) | | | (M) | (M) | | | (M) | | (L) | (M) | ↓↓ | |
| I B | Lidocaine (Xylocaine) | B | | (L) | | | | | | (L) | (M) | | |
| | Mexiletine (Mexitil) | | | (L) | | | | | | (L) | (M) | | |
| I C | Propafenone (Rythmol) | C | | (B) | | | (M) | | | (M) | (L) | ↓↓ | ↓ |
| | Flecainide (Tambocor) | | | (B) | | | | | | (H) | (L) | ↓↓ | |
| II | β-Adrenergic antagonists | | | | | | (H) | | | (L) | (L) | ↓ | ↓↓ |
| III | Dronedarone (Multaq) | | (L) | (L) | (H) | (M) | (M) | (M) | | (L) | (H) | ↓ | ↓ |
| | Amiodarone (Cordarone) | | (L) | (L) | (H) | (M) | (M) | (M) | | (L) | (H) | | ↓ |
| | Sotalol (Betapace) | | | | (H) | | (H) | | | (H) | (L) | ↓ | ↓ |
| | Ibutilide (Corvert) | | | △ | (H) | | | | | (H) | (L) | | |
| | Dofetilide (Tikosyn) | | | | (H) | | | | | (H) | (L) | | |
| IV | Verapamil (Calan, Isoptin) | | (M) | | | | | | | (L) | (L) | ↓↓ | ↓ |
| | Diltiazem (Cardizem) | | (M) | | | | | | | (L) | (L) | ↓ | ↓ |
| Misc | Adenosine (Adenocard) | | | | | | | | △ | (L) | (L) | | ↓ |

| Antagonist relative potency | △ = Agonist |
|---|---|
| L = Low | ● = ECG Changes related to Ca$^{++}$ channel block |
| M = Moderate | ● = ECG Changes related to Na$^+$ channel block |
| H = High | ● = ECG Changes related to K$^+$ channel block |

## 4.6 Hypertrophy Patterns

### 4.6.1 Left Ventricular Hypertrophy (LVH)

**Characteristics:**

- Increased QRS voltage (e.g., S wave in V1 + R wave in V5 or V6 >35 mm).
- Left axis deviation.
- ST-segment depression and T-wave inversion in left-sided leads (strain pattern).

**Significance:**

- Associated with hypertension, aortic stenosis, and hypertrophic cardiomyopathy.

### 4.6.2 Right Ventricular Hypertrophy (RVH)

**Characteristics:**

- Right axis deviation.

- R wave greater than S wave in V1.
- Deep S wave in V6.

**Significance:**

- Associated with pulmonary hypertension, chronic lung disease, and congenital heart disease.

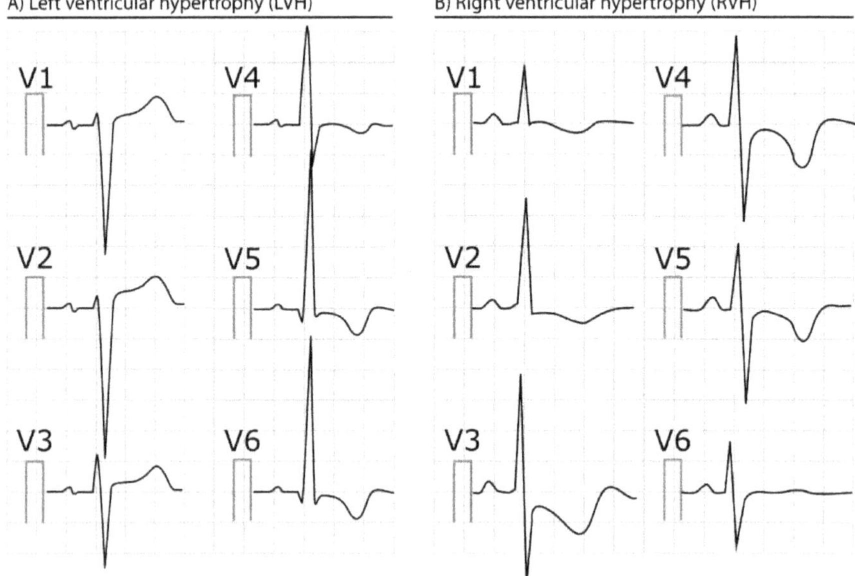


## 4.7 Miscellaneous Conditions

### 4.7.1 Pericarditis

**Characteristics:**

- Diffuse ST-segment elevation
    - PR-segment depression.

**Significance:**

- Inflammation of the pericardium often due to infection, autoimmune disease, or post-myocardial infarction.

### 4.7.2 Pulmonary Embolism

**Characteristics:**

- S1Q3T3 pattern (deep S wave in lead I, Q wave and inverted T wave in lead III).
- Right axis deviation.
- Right bundle branch block.

**Significance:**

- Life-threatening condition requiring immediate treatment with anticoagulation and possible thrombolysis.

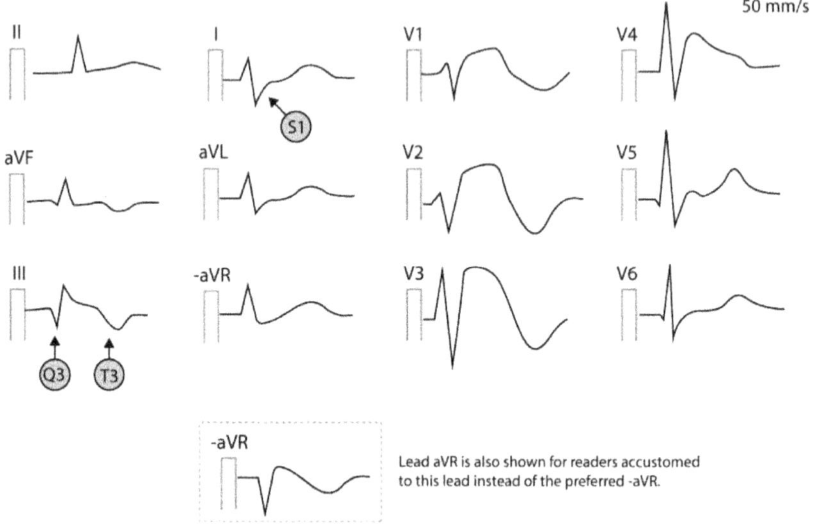


## 4.8 Conclusion

Recognizing and understanding abnormal ECG patterns are essential for the timely diagnosis and management of various cardiac conditions. Mastery of ECG interpretation allows healthcare professionals to quickly identify life-threatening arrhythmias, conduction disturbances, myocardial infarctions, electrolyte imbalances, and other critical conditions, ultimately improving patient outcomes in emergency settings.

# CHAPTER SIX

# ECG INTERPRETATION IN CLINICAL PRACTICE

ECG interpretation is a fundamental skill in clinical practice, especially in emergency settings where timely and accurate diagnosis is crucial. This chapter outlines a systematic approach to ECG interpretation, including key steps, common pitfalls, and practical tips for effective analysis.

### 5.1 Systematic Approach to ECG Interpretation

A structured approach to ECG interpretation ensures that all aspects of the ECG are reviewed systematically, minimizing the risk of missing critical abnormalities. The following steps are commonly used in clinical practice:

1. Verify Patient Details
- Confirm patient identity, age, and clinical context.
- Ensure the ECG is properly labeled with patient information and time of recording.

2. Assess ECG Quality
- Check the calibration (standard: 10 mm/mV, 25 mm/sec paper speed).
- Verify lead placement and signal quality.
- Ensure there is minimal artifact or interference.

3. Determine Heart Rate
- **Regular Rhythm:** Count the number of large squares between R-R intervals and use the formula

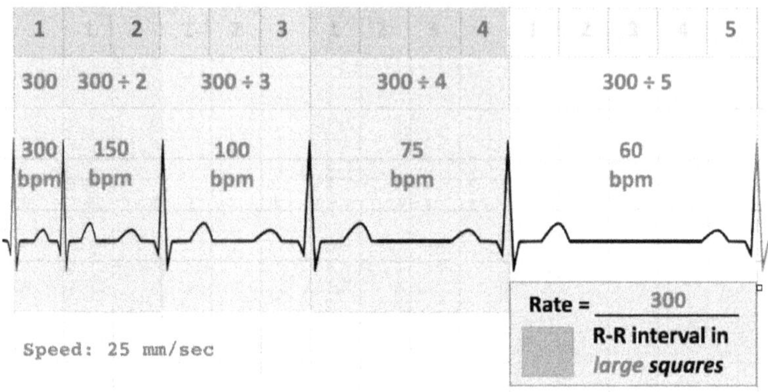


- **Irregular Rhythm:** Use the 6-second strip method by counting the number of R waves in a 6-second segment and multiplying by 10.

4. Analyze the Rhythm

- **Identify the P Waves:** Determine if each P wave is followed by a QRS complex. Assess P wave morphology and consistency.

- **Measure the PR Interval:** Verify if it falls within the normal range (0.12 to 0.20 seconds). Prolongation or shortening can indicate conduction abnormalities.

- **Evaluate the QRS Complex:** Check for duration (normal: 0.06 to 0.10 seconds) and morphology. Look for widened QRS complexes or abnormal patterns.

- **Inspect the ST Segment:** Ensure it is isoelectric. Look for elevations or depressions which can indicate ischemia or infarction.

- **Assess the T Waves:** Evaluate their shape, direction, and amplitude. Abnormalities can indicate electrolyte imbalances or ischemia.

- **Measure the QT Interval:** Correct for heart rate if needed. Prolongation or shortening can be significant for arrhythmia risk.

- **Look for U Waves:** Note their presence and significance, if applicable.

5. Analyze the Axis

- **Determine the Cardiac Axis:** Use the limb leads to assess the heart's electrical axis. Normal axis ranges from -30° to +90°.

- **Identify Deviations:** Left or right axis deviation can indicate underlying conditions such as hypertrophy or conduction abnormalities.

6. Identify and Interpret Abnormalities

- **Arrhythmias:** Recognize patterns such as atrial fibrillation, ventricular tachycardia, and other arrhythmias.

- **Conduction Abnormalities:** Detect blocks such as first-degree, second-degree, or third-degree AV blocks, and bundle branch blocks.

- **Ischemia and Infarction:** Identify ST-segment elevations or depressions, pathological Q waves, and T-wave inversions indicative of myocardial infarction.

- **Electrolyte Imbalances:** Look for changes consistent with hyperkalemia, hypokalemia, hypercalcemia, and hypocalcemia.

   7. Correlate with Clinical Findings

- Integrate ECG findings with the patient's clinical presentation, history, and symptoms.

- Consider differential diagnoses and further diagnostic testing if necessary.

### 5.2 Common Pitfalls in ECG Interpretation

### 1. Misinterpreting Artifact as Pathology

- **Pitfall:** Movement, poor electrode contact, or external interference can mimic pathological changes.

- **Solution:** Ensure good electrode placement and repeat the ECG if necessary. Identify and distinguish artifacts from true abnormalities.

### 2. Overlooking Subtle Changes

- **Pitfall:** Small deviations from normal can be missed, leading to missed diagnoses.

- **Solution:** Use systematic analysis to detect subtle changes, and consider repeating the ECG or comparing with previous tracings if needed.

### 3. Relying Solely on Automated Interpretation

- **Pitfall:** ECG machines often provide automated interpretations that may not be accurate.

- **Solution:** Always review the ECG manually and consider the clinical context, as automated readings can sometimes be incorrect or incomplete.

### 4. Failing to Consider Clinical Context

- **Pitfall:** ECG findings may be misinterpreted without considering the patient's clinical history and symptoms.

- **Solution:** Correlate ECG findings with the patient's presentation, and avoid jumping to conclusions without full context.

### 5.3 Practical Tips for Effective ECG Interpretation

### 1. Practice Regularly

- Regular practice helps in recognizing normal and abnormal patterns more efficiently.

- Use practice ECGs and case studies to improve diagnostic skills.

### 2. Use a Systematic Approach

- Adhere to a consistent method for analyzing ECGs to ensure no aspects are overlooked.

- Consider using mnemonics or checklists to guide the interpretation process.

### 3. Consult Resources and Colleagues

- Use reference materials, such as textbooks and online resources, for complex cases.

- Consult with colleagues or specialists if uncertain about a diagnosis.

### 4. Stay Updated with Guidelines

- Keep abreast of updates and changes in ECG interpretation guidelines and best practices.

- Participate in continuing education and training opportunities.

### 5. Document Findings Thoroughly

- Ensure comprehensive documentation of ECG findings, interpretations, and clinical correlations.

- This is crucial for accurate patient records and continuity of care.

### 6. Integrate with Other Diagnostic Tools

- Combine ECG findings with other diagnostic modalities, such as echocardiography, stress tests, and blood tests, for a comprehensive assessment.

### 5.4 Case Studies and Practical Applications

### 1. Case Study: Acute Myocardial Infarction

- **Presentation:** Patient with chest pain and dyspnea.

- **ECG Findings:** ST-segment elevation in leads II, III, and aVF.

- **Interpretation:** Inferior STEMI. Immediate reperfusion therapy required.

### 2. Case Study: Atrial Fibrillation

- **Presentation:** Patient with palpitations and fatigue.

- **ECG Findings:** Irregularly irregular rhythm with no distinct P waves.

- **Interpretation:** Atrial fibrillation. Assess for anticoagulation and rate control.

### 3. Case Study: Hyperkalemia

- **Presentation:** Patient with muscle weakness and renal failure.

- **ECG Findings:** Peaked T waves, widened QRS complex.

- **Interpretation:** Hyperkalemia. Initiate treatment with calcium gluconate and address the underlying cause.

### 4. Case Study: Bundle Branch Block

- **Presentation:** Patient with syncope and fatigue.
- **ECG Findings:** Wide QRS complex with characteristic RSR' pattern in V1.
- **Interpretation:** Right bundle branch block. Evaluate for associated conditions and symptoms.

### 5.5 Conclusion

Effective ECG interpretation is a critical skill in emergency care and clinical practice. By applying a systematic approach, recognizing common pitfalls, and correlating findings with clinical context, healthcare professionals can enhance their diagnostic accuracy and improve patient outcomes. Continuous practice and staying updated with guidelines and best practices are essential for maintaining proficiency in ECG interpretation.

# CHAPTER SEVEN

# AXIS

The electrical axis of the heart is an essential aspect of ECG interpretation. It represents the direction of the net electrical activity of the heart during ventricular depolarization. Understanding and analyzing the ECG axis can help diagnose various cardiac conditions and deviations. This chapter provides a comprehensive overview of ECG axis determination, normal ranges, and clinical implications of axis deviations.

## 6.1 Understanding the Cardiac Axis

**1. Definition:**

- The cardiac axis refers to the general direction of the electrical impulses as they travel through the heart. It is primarily determined by analyzing the QRS complex in the limb leads.

**2. Importance:**

- The axis helps identify normal electrical activity and deviations, which can be indicative of underlying heart conditions such as hypertrophy, conduction abnormalities, or myocardial infarction.

**3. Determination:**

- The axis is determined by examining the QRS complex in the frontal plane leads (I, II, III, aVL, aVR, aVF). The electrical axis is typically measured in degrees and can be visualized on a hexaxial reference system.

## 6.2 Normal ECG Axis

**1. Normal Range:**

- The normal electrical axis of the heart ranges from -30° to +90°.

- **Average Axis:** Approximately +60°.

**2. Hexaxial Reference System:**

- The hexaxial reference system is a circle divided into 360 degrees, representing the frontal plane. Leads I, II, and III are positioned at 0°, +60°, and +120° respectively. Leads aVR, aVL, and aVF are positioned at -150°,

-30°, and +90° respectively.

    3. Identifying the Normal Axis:

- In a normal axis, the QRS complexes in lead I and lead aVF will both be positive.

- The QRS complex will be positive in leads I and aVF, with no significant deviation in the axis.

| Lead 1 | Lead aVF | Quadrant | Axis |
|---|---|---|---|
| POSITIVE | POSITIVE |  | **Normal Axis** (0 to +90°) |
| POSITIVE | **NEGATIVE** |  | ****Possible LAD** (0 to -90°) |
| **NEGATIVE** | POSITIVE |  | **RAD** (+90° to 180°) |
| **NEGATIVE** | **NEGATIVE** |  | **Extreme Axis** (-90° to 180°) |

## 6.3 Determining the Cardiac Axis

    1. Identify the QRS Complex Polarity in Limb Leads:

- Lead I: If the QRS is positive, the axis is more towards the left; if negative, the axis is more towards the right.

- Lead aVF: If the QRS is positive, the axis is directed downward; if negative, the axis is directed upward.

    2. Use the Quadrant Method:

- **Normal Axis (0° to +90°):** Positive QRS in leads I and aVF.

- **Left Axis Deviation (LAD, -30° to -90°):** Positive QRS in lead I and negative QRS in aVF.

- **Right Axis Deviation (RAD, +90° to +180°):** Positive QRS in aVF and negative QRS in lead I.

- **Extreme Axis Deviation (-90° to -180° or +180° to +360°):** Negative QRS in both leads I and aVF.

3. Degree Calculation:

- **Use the Vector Analysis:** By plotting the QRS amplitude in leads I and aVF, the axis can be determined using vector analysis or ECG axis calculators.

- **Example:** If the QRS is positive in lead I and negative in lead aVF, the axis is in the left quadrant (LAD). If the QRS is positive in lead aVF and negative in lead I, the axis is in the right quadrant (RAD).

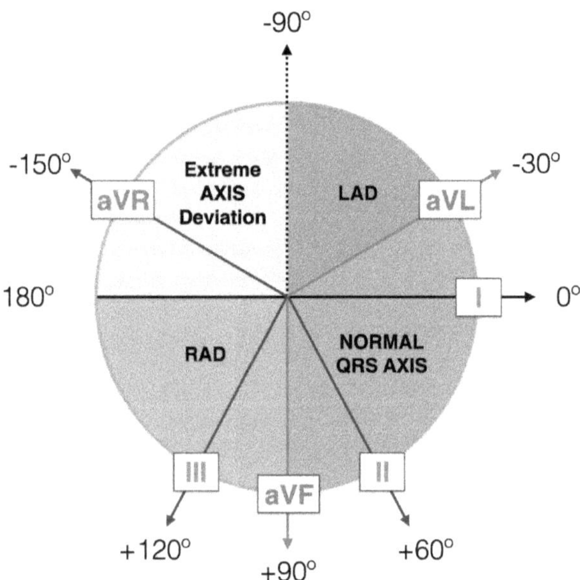


## 6.4 Clinical Significance of Axis Deviations

1. Left Axis Deviation (LAD):

- Characteristics: QRS complex is positive in lead I and negative in lead aVF, with an axis generally between -30° and -90°.

- Potential Causes:

- Left ventricular hypertrophy (LVH).

- Left anterior fascicular block.

- Inferior myocardial infarction.

- Hyperkalemia.

- *Clinical Relevance:* LAD can indicate cardiac stress or pathology and may warrant further investigation for underlying causes.

2. Right Axis Deviation (RAD):
- Characteristics: QRS complex is positive in lead aVF and negative in lead I, with an axis generally between +90° and +180°.
- Potential Causes:
- Right ventricular hypertrophy (RVH).
- Left posterior fascicular block.
- Chronic obstructive pulmonary disease (COPD).
- Acute pulmonary embolism.
- *Clinical Relevance:* RAD can indicate conditions affecting the right side of the heart or pulmonary circulation and may require additional evaluation.

3. Extreme Axis Deviation:
- Characteristics: QRS complex is negative in both lead I and lead aVF, with an axis between -90° and -180° or +180° and +360°.
- Potential Causes:
- Severe cardiac abnormalities.
- Ventricular tachycardia.
- Lead misplacement or incorrect ECG interpretation.
- *Clinical Relevance:* Extreme axis deviation is often associated with serious cardiac conditions and requires prompt evaluation and intervention.

### 6.5 Case Studies and Practical Applications

**1. Case Study: Left Axis Deviation**
- **Presentation:** Patient with symptoms of heart failure and suspected LVH.
- **ECG Findings:** Positive QRS in lead I and negative QRS in lead aVF.
- **Interpretation:** Left axis deviation. Consider further assessment for LVH and possible echocardiography.

**2. Case Study: Right Axis Deviation**
- **Presentation:** Patient with shortness of breath and suspected pulmonary embolism.
- **ECG Findings:** Positive QRS in lead aVF and negative QRS in lead I.
- **Interpretation:** Right axis deviation. Evaluate for possible pulmonary embolism and right heart strain.

**3. Case Study: Extreme Axis Deviation**
- **Presentation:** Patient with syncope and tachycardia.
- **ECG Findings:** Negative QRS in both lead I and lead aVF.
- **Interpretation:** Extreme axis deviation. Assess for potential ventricular tachycardia and verify lead placement.

## <u>6.6 Conclusion</u>

Accurate determination of the ECG axis is crucial for diagnosing various cardiac conditions and guiding clinical decision-making. By understanding the normal axis, applying systematic methods to determine deviations, and correlating findings with clinical context, healthcare professionals can enhance their diagnostic accuracy and improve patient care in emergency and clinical settings.

# CHAPTER EIGHT

# ECG IN SPECIAL POPULATION

ECG interpretation can vary significantly across different patient populations due to physiological differences, underlying conditions, and clinical scenarios. This chapter explores how ECG patterns may differ in various special populations, including pediatric patients, elderly individuals, pregnant women, athletes, and patients with specific medical conditions.

### 7.1 Pediatric Patients

**1. Normal Pediatric ECG Characteristics:**

- **Heart Rate:** Faster in infants and young children compared to adults. Rates can range from 120 to 160 beats per minute in newborns and decrease with age.
- **P Waves:** May be more variable in shape compared to adults. Atrial rates may be faster in young children.
- **QRS Complex:** Narrower and shorter in duration. Pediatric patients often have a higher heart rate and more pronounced R waves in V1 and V2.
- **ST Segment and T Waves:** T-wave inversions may be normal in some leads in infants and children.

**2. Common Abnormalities:**

- **Premature Ventricular Contractions (PVCs):** May be seen more frequently in children and can be benign.
- **Congenital Heart Defects:** Conditions like Tetralogy of Fallot or ventricular septal defects can manifest with specific ECG findings.
- **Prolonged QT Interval:** Can be congenital or due to medication effects; requires careful evaluation and management.

**3. Clinical Considerations:**

- Always correlate ECG findings with clinical presentation and history.

- Pediatric ECGs should be interpreted in the context of age-specific norms and developmental changes.

### 7.2 Elderly Patients

**1. Normal Age-Related Changes:**

- **Heart Rate:** May be lower due to decreased autonomic responsiveness.
- **P Waves:** P wave changes, including a longer PR interval, may occur due to age-related conduction changes.
- **QRS Complex:** QRS duration may increase due to age-related changes in conduction system integrity.
- **ST Segment and T Waves:** ST-segment depression and T-wave changes can be more common due to age-related ischemic changes or cardiac remodeling.

**2. Common Abnormalities:**

- **Atrial Fibrillation:** Higher prevalence in the elderly due to age-related structural changes in the heart.
- **Bundle Branch Blocks:** Increased incidence of left and right bundle branch blocks with age.
- **Heart Failure:** ECG changes consistent with heart failure may include widened QRS complexes and left axis deviation.

**3. Clinical Considerations:**

- Elderly patients may have multiple comorbid conditions affecting ECG interpretation.
- Consider the potential for atypical presentations of ischemia and infarction in this age group.

### 7.3 Pregnant Women

**1. Normal Pregnancy-Related ECG Changes:**

- **Heart Rate:** Typically increased by 10-20 beats per minute due to increased cardiac output.
- **P Waves:** May be more prominent due to increased blood volume and cardiac workload.
- **QRS Complex:** QRS axis may shift slightly due to changes in thoracic anatomy.
- **ST Segment and T Waves:** Mild ST-segment elevation may occur in the third trimester; usually benign.

**2. Common Abnormalities:**

- **Sinus Tachycardia:** Common due to increased cardiac output.
- **Physiological Left Axis Deviation:** Can occur due to the shifting of the heart position.

- **Preeclampsia and Eclampsia:** Can cause changes in the ECG such as ST-segment changes and T-wave inversions due to altered cardiovascular function.

### 3. Clinical Considerations:
- Correlate ECG findings with gestational age and the presence of symptoms.
- Consider potential for normal physiological changes versus pathological conditions.

### 7.4 Athletes

### 1. Normal Athletic Heart Adaptations:
- **Heart Rate:** Bradycardia is common in athletes, reflecting high cardiac efficiency.
- **P Waves:** May show slight variations due to increased vagal tone.
- **QRS Complex:** Increased voltage due to left ventricular hypertrophy; QRS duration may be normal or slightly increased.
- **ST Segment and T Waves:** ST-segment elevation and T-wave changes in precordial leads can be normal.

### 2. Common Abnormalities:
- **Athlete's Heart Syndrome:** Benign findings include increased QRS voltage and ST-segment changes.
- **Arrhythmias:** Athletes may experience occasional benign arrhythmias such as atrial premature beats; however, persistent arrhythmias should be evaluated.

### 3. Clinical Considerations:
- Distinguish between benign adaptations of the athletic heart and pathological conditions.
- Ensure thorough evaluation if there are symptoms such as syncope or palpitations.

### 7.5 Patients with Specific Medical Conditions

### 1. Diabetes Mellitus:
- **Normal Changes:** ECG may show increased risk of ischemia and altered T-wave morphology.
- **Common Abnormalities:** Increased risk of coronary artery disease, leading to ST-segment changes or T-wave inversions.
- **Clinical Considerations:** Regular monitoring and management of cardiovascular risk factors are essential.

### 2. Chronic Obstructive Pulmonary Disease (COPD):
- **Normal Changes:** May show right axis deviation and signs of right

ventricular strain.

- **Common Abnormalities:** ECG findings may include tall R waves in V1 and right bundle branch block.

- **Clinical Considerations:** Correlate ECG findings with respiratory status and other diagnostic tests.

### 3. Renal Failure:

- **Normal Changes:** Electrolyte imbalances in renal failure can cause significant ECG changes.

- **Common Abnormalities:** Hyperkalemia may cause peaked T waves, widened QRS complexes, and sine wave patterns.

- **Clinical Considerations:** Immediate treatment of electrolyte imbalances is crucial; ECG changes should be monitored closely.

### 4. Hyperthyroidism and Hypothyroidism:

- **Hyperthyroidism:** May cause sinus tachycardia, atrial fibrillation, and ST-segment changes.

- **Hypothyroidism:** May show bradycardia, prolonged QT interval, and low-voltage complexes.

- **Clinical Considerations:** Address thyroid dysfunction as part of the treatment plan.

### 5. Myocarditis and Pericarditis:

- **Myocarditis:** May present with ST-segment elevation and T-wave changes.

- **Pericarditis:** Typically shows diffuse ST-segment elevation and PR-segment depression.

- **Clinical Considerations:** Correlate with clinical symptoms and other diagnostic findings.

### 7.6 Conclusion

Understanding ECG interpretation in special populations requires a nuanced approach, considering the physiological changes and specific clinical scenarios associated with each group. By recognizing normal variations and potential abnormalities, healthcare professionals can better interpret ECGs and make informed decisions about patient management. Careful correlation with clinical context and ongoing evaluation are essential for accurate diagnosis and optimal patient care.

# CHAPTER NINE

# CONCLUSION

This book, *ECG for Emergency*, aims to provide a comprehensive guide to understanding and applying ECG principles in emergency settings, ensuring that healthcare professionals can make timely and informed decisions.

Throughout this book, we have explored the fundamental aspects of ECG interpretation, including the basics of ECG waveform analysis, lead placement, and the identification of normal and abnormal patterns. We delved into the specific considerations for special populations, such as pediatric patients, the elderly, pregnant women, athletes, and those with chronic conditions, recognizing that each group presents unique challenges and variations in ECG readings.

The exploration of common and critical abnormalities—ranging from arrhythmias and myocardial infarctions to electrolyte imbalances and structural heart changes—underscores the importance of a systematic and nuanced approach to ECG interpretation. Mastery of these concepts is crucial not only for accurate diagnosis but also for effective management and treatment in emergency scenarios.

Furthermore, the case studies and practical applications included in this book illustrate real-world scenarios and reinforce the importance of correlating ECG findings with clinical context. This integration of theory and practice ensures that readers can confidently apply their knowledge to diverse clinical situations, enhancing their diagnostic and therapeutic capabilities.

In conclusion, the ECG is a powerful tool that, when understood and utilized effectively, can significantly impact patient outcomes in emergency settings. This book serves as a foundation for developing expertise in ECG interpretation, contributing to better clinical decision-making and ultimately, improved patient care.

We hope this guide serves as a valuable resource in your journey to mastering ECG interpretation in emergency care, and we encourage continuous learning and application of these principles to meet the ever-evolving demands of the field.

Thank You...

Dr. Charan S Yelanadu

*"Love for General Medicine....."*

# References

1. Books and Textbooks
- **Dubin, D.** (2014). *Rapid Interpretation of EKG's*. 7<sup>th</sup> Edition. Cover Publishing.
- A classic resource providing a comprehensive yet accessible approach to ECG interpretation.
- **Kligfield, P., Gettes, L. S., Bailey, J. J., et al.** (2007). *The Precordial Leads: Placement and Configuration.* In *The ECG in Emergency Medicine and Acute Care*. Cambridge University Press.
- Detailed information on lead placement and configuration in emergency settings.
- **Wagner, G. S.** (2014). *Williams Textbook of Endocrinology*. 13<sup>th</sup> Edition. Elsevier.
- An authoritative source on ECG changes associated with various endocrine disorders.
    2. Guidelines and Recommendations
- **American Heart Association.** (2021). *2021 AHA Guidelines for CPR and ECC*. Circulation, 144(8_suppl_2), S1-S60. https://doi.org/10.1161/CIR.0000000000000948
- Provides updated guidelines for CPR, including ECG interpretation in emergency situations.
- **European Society of Cardiology.** (2019). *2019 ESC Guidelines for the diagnosis and management of acute myocardial infarction in patients presenting with ST-segment elevation*. European Heart Journal, 40(3), 259-315. https://doi.org/10.1093/eurheartj/ehz456
- Offers guidelines for diagnosing and managing ST-segment elevation myocardial infarction (STEMI).
    3. Journal Articles
- **Jentzer, J. C., & Body, R.** (2020). *ECG in Emergency Medicine: Current Concepts and Future Directions*. Emergency Medicine Clinics of North America, 38(1), 123-139. https://doi.org/10.1016/j.emc.2019.09.005
- An overview of current concepts and future directions in ECG interpretation for emergency medicine.
- **Kotecha, D., & Kotecha, S.** (2019). *The role of ECG in the diagnosis and management of atrial fibrillation*. Heart, 105(22), 1750-1756.

https://doi.org/10.1136/heartjnl-2019-315946

- Discusses the use of ECG for diagnosing and managing atrial fibrillation.

4. Online Resources

- **Mayo Clinic.** (2022). *Electrocardiogram (ECG or EKG)*. https://www.mayoclinic.org/tests-procedures/ecg/about/ pac-20385020

- A reliable source for understanding the basics of ECG and its clinical applications.

- **UpToDate.** (2023). *ECG Interpretation: An Overview*. https://www.uptodate.com/contents/ecg-interpretation-an-overview

- A comprehensive overview of ECG interpretation available through UpToDate.

5. Special Populations and Case Studies

- **Agarwal, S. K., & Jorgensen, L. R.** (2018). *ECG changes in athletes: Differentiating physiological adaptations from pathological conditions*. Current Sports Medicine Reports, 17(5), 165-173. https://doi.org/ 10.1249/JSR.0000000000000503

- Discusses the physiological and pathological ECG changes observed in athletes.

- **Nakai, H., & Okada, Y.** (2020). *ECG findings in pregnant women: A review of the literature*. International Journal of Cardiology, 308, 30-35. https://doi.org/10.1016/j.ijcard.2020.02.051

- Reviews ECG findings and changes during pregnancy, with a focus on clinical implications.